CW00702617

PORTRAIT OF THE PENNINES

JOHN MORRISON

HALSGROVE

Dedicated to Glyn Hughes, a man of the Pennines

First published in Great Britain in 2008

British Library Cataloguing-in-Publication Data
A CIP record for this title is available from the British Library

ISBN 978 1 84114 739 0

HALSGROVE
Halsgrove House
Ryelands Industrial Estate
Bagley Road, Wellington, Somerset TA21 9PZ
Tel: 01823 653777 Fax: 01823 216796
email: sales@halsgrove.com
website: www.halsgrove.com

Printed and bound by
Grafiche Flaminia, Italy

INTRODUCTION

People don't generally go to a place called 'the Pennines'. They go to picnic in the delectable limestone dales of Derbyshire, where the rivers run as clear as when Isaak Walton first tried his luck with rod and line. They lace up their walking boots and follow in the footsteps of Benny Rothman and his pals, whose mass trespass on Kinder Scout back in 1932 led to many tracts of hitherto private upland being opened up. They lengthen their stride across the South Pennine moors that were so familiar to the precociously talented Brontë sisters.

They explore the dales of Yorkshire, from the lush Wharfe valley to the lead mines of Upper Swaledale. Pennine Wayfarers stagger across featureless Stainmore, and admire the view from the top of Cross Fell, buffeted by a fierce, localised wind known as the Helm. They accompany the wall, built to repel Scottish raiders and to mark the limit of Hadrian's imperial ambitions. And when they visit these fascinating places, it's a Pennine landscape that they see.

The Pennines are the backbone of England, the watershed of our northern counties. Two drops of water from a single rain shower in the Yorkshire Dales, falling either side of the watershed, will take very different courses. One drop will join the River Wharfe, flowing 75 miles through the Dales to Cawood, merging with the waters of the Swale, Ure and Nidd to become the River Ouse, which decants, via the Humber Estuary, into the North Sea. The other drop will find the River Ribble and flow across the plain of Lancashire to meet the Irish Sea. For reasons I'm still not too sure about, I find this utterly amazing.

The Pennines are too big to take in all at once... in length if not in height. Arguably, only those hardy souls who have trudged every foot-slogging mile of the Pennine Way, from Edale to Kirk Yetholm, have a full appreciation of just how far they extend. It's well-nigh impossible to draw a definitive boundary to show where the Pennines begin and where they end. So I'm happy to default to the map in W A Poucher's book, *The Backbone of England*. The Pennine effect is accumulative, with no peak standing head-and-shoulder above its neighbours. Summits are gently rounded, unlike craggy Lakeland peaks. Walkers would be unlikely to guess that Cross Fell (at 893 metres) and Whernside (at 737 metres and often likened, in shape, to a beached whale) are the highest points of the Pennines and Yorkshire respectively.

Away from the watershed, the Pennine landscape offers tremendous variety (though try telling that to a walker trudging through blanket bog on Bleaklow or Black Hill!). Fertile valleys are divided up by a patchwork of dry stone walls, and backed up by heather moorland and sheep-cropped fells. Limestone has created the steep-sided dales of Derbyshire's White Peak, the fascinating 'pavements' of the Yorkshire Dales and the theatricality of Malham Cove. The Dark Peak offers a harsher landscape, where gritstone is weathered into fantastic shapes and walkers question their sanity.

Poucher draws a veil over the industrial heartlands of the South Pennines. Of course, at the time he was writing, the mill chimneys were still casting palls of smoke into the valleys, so perhaps he can be forgiven. Between the milltowns of East Lancashire and West Yorkshire lie some of the finest walking country in the North.

For centuries travellers visited the Pennines merely to get from one side to the other, a crossing that held many terrors from inhospitable terrain and weather. Canals were built across the Pennines, at their lowest points. Railway lines were tunnelled through hills, spanning valleys on massive viaducts. These enterprises represented the cutting edge of civil engineering during the eighteenth and nineteenth centuries. Only with the building of the M62 motorway could we say that the terrors of trans-Pennine travel had been conquered.

The photographs follow a logical progression, from south to north, beginning with the Derbyshire Dales and ending at Hadrian's Wall. My apologies if your favourite landmark isn't featured here. I wanted to give a full flavour of the Pennine landscape, not just a gazeteer of the best-known beauty spots. I shoot what I call 'emotional landscapes' – trying to show not just what a place *looks* like, but what it *feels* like too. I've enjoyed being out in all weathers, at dawn and dusk, with light chasing shadows across the Pennine hills. I hope you enjoy the journey too.

John Morrison
hurlmere@btinternet.com
www.northpic.co.uk

Bishopdale.

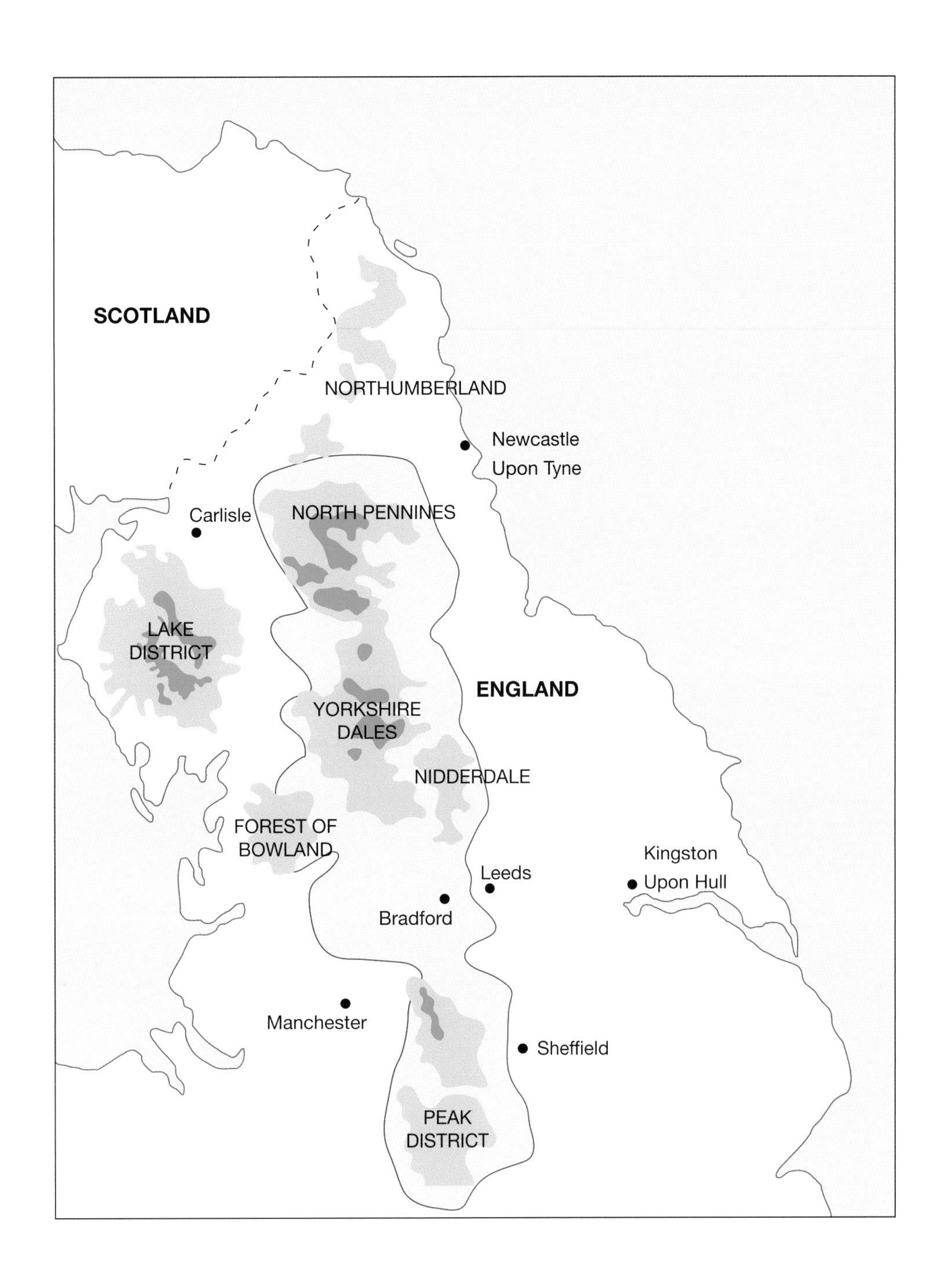
SCOTLAND
NORTHUMBERLAND
Newcastle
Upon Tyne
Carlisle
NORTH PENNINES
LAKE
DISTRICT
ENGLAND
YORKSHIRE
DALES
NIDDERDALE
FOREST OF
BOWLAND
Kingston
Upon Hull
Leeds
Bradford
Manchester
Sheffield
PEAK
DISTRICT

Wildflower meadow near Longnor, in Derbyshire's White Peak, backed up by symmetrical fields.

Izaak Walton, author of *The Compleat Angler*, declared the River Lathkill to be 'the purest and most transparent' he ever saw.

Above: Fernilee Reservoir, in the Goyt Valley, on the border between Derbyshire and Cheshire.

Left: A shallow wier on the River Dove, which meanders through the limestone scenery of Dovedale.

Downy clouds and soft light as dawn comes to a typical Peak District pasture.

The sharp, distinctive outline of Parkhouse Hill, south of Buxton.

Traffic heading west out of Castleton has to negotiate the steep limestone gorge of Winnats Pass.

The paved path to the top of Mam Tor, which overlooks both Edale and the Hope Valley.

Hope Valley Cement Works, next to a limestone quarry; to the north is gritstone country, known as the Dark Peak.

The Edale Valley – and the plateau of Kinder Scout – seen from the flank of Mam Tor.

A fist of weathered rock overlooks Grindsbrook Clough, at the start of the Pennine Way.

Rock 'sculptures' on the edge of Kinder Scout create intriguing silhouettes.

Above: In 1932 a band of ramblers dared to trespass on Kinder Scout – an event that helped to open up the northern hills to walkers.

Right: A happy geological accident: an old couple, puckering up on Bleaklow.

Above: Hay-time creates patterns in fields near Slaithwaite.

Left: Into West Yorkshire, as a shaft of sunlight picks out fields near Huddersfield.

Above: The start of a memorable balloon trip, from Castle Hill, near Huddersfield.

Right: Windfarms divide opinions like no other features in the landscape.

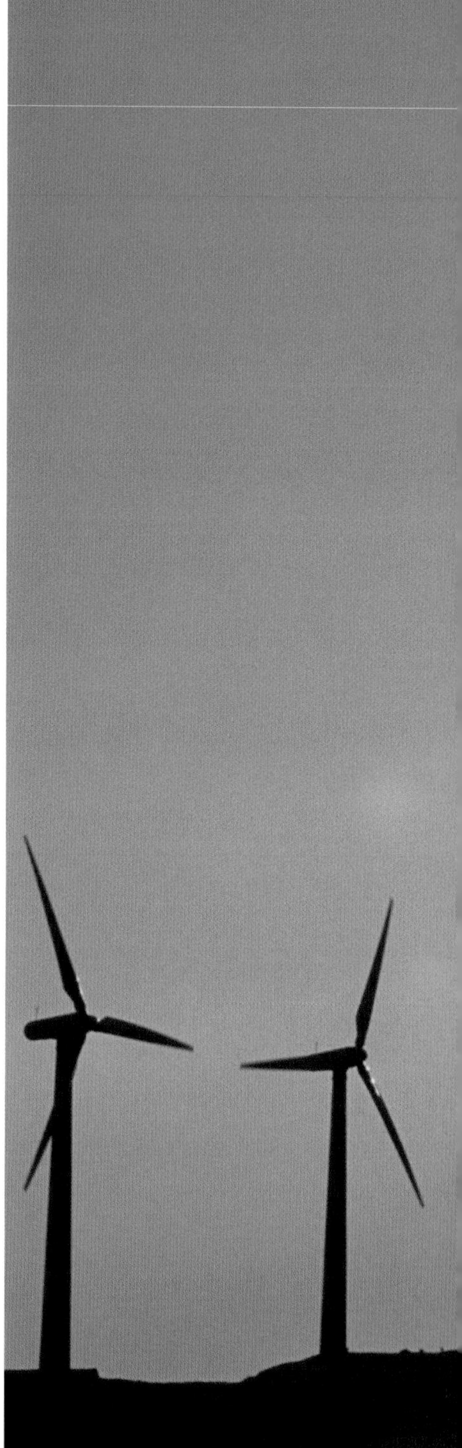

A wintry scene near Diggle, just over the county border in Lancashire.

The bridestones, above Todmorden, offer more natural sculptures.

Above: Todmorden, where road, rail, river and canal are shoehorned into a narrow valley.

Left: Coal Clough Windfarm, harvesting strong breezes on a South Pennine hillside.

A view of Halifax from Beacon Hill: a view no longer hidden by palls of smoke from mill chimneys.

A walker leaves Todmorden behind by following a line of causeway stones, once used by strings of packhorses.

Above: Sowerby Bridge, another town where mills, houses, pubs and chapels were squeezed into every patch of available land.

Left: Above the milltowns of West Yorkshire, the moorland landscape stretches to the horizon.

The woodland setting of Gibson Mill, in Hardcastle Crags, where the workforce included young children.

Lined up: a South Pennine farmhouse, Heptonstall church tower and the ubiquitous landmark of Stoodley Pike.

A pair of geese pose on the towpath of the Rochdale Canal at Hebden Bridge.

When there was no space left in the valley at Hebden Bridge, houses were built up the steep hillside.

Heptonstall in winter: a fine example of a hilltop village.

Redundant mills and new houses: the changing face of the South Pennines.

Above: A farmhouse in Crimsworth Dene, long abandoned to wind and weather.

Left: Sailboats pirouette on the burnished waters of Warley Moor Reservoir.

A scene the Brontës knew well, since Haworth Parsonage looked out across the graveyard.

A foggy day in Haworth: another scene the Brontë sisters would recognise.

The old road from Hebden Bridge to Haworth, where it meets the Pennine Way.

Pendle Hill, one of the Pennines' outlying hills, viewed from Boulsworth Hill.

A steam train pulls in at Oakworth, one of the stations on the Keighley and Worth Valley Railway.

East Riddlesden Hall, near Keighley, one of Pennine Yorkshire's gaunt, gritstone 'Halifax houses'.

Dry stone walls divide the landscape around Cowling into a patchwork of fields.

The Cow and Calf rocks, overlooking the spa town of Ilkey and the valley of the Wharfe.

Pancake Rock on Ilkey Moor, an expanse of heather moorland where the millhands of Bradford found fresh air and freedom.

A quartet of climbers prepare to tackle a rockface at the Cow and Calf rocks.

The Leeds and Liverpool Canal follows the 'Aire Gap', a break in the Pennine hills where milltowns give way to the Yorkshire Dales.

Negotiating a lock on the Leeds and Liverpool Canal near Barnoldswick.

Above: Sheep farming is an important part of the rural economy in the Pennine uplands.

Left: An old milestone offers directions to both Skipton and Addingham.

The village green at Ramsgill, a tiny community in Nidderdale.

Above: A walker silhouetted against a dramatic sky at the Chevin, a well-known viewpoint overlooking the Wharfe Valley.

Right: Brimham Rocks, near Pateley Bridge: outcrops of millstone grit, eroded into fantastic shapes during the last ice age.

The Dancing Bear, one of the weathered 'sculptures' at Brimham Rocks.

Limestone country once again: a limestone pavement near Threshfield.

Trees that seem to tell a story – and not a very happy one – near Hellifield.

The Leeds and Liverpool Canal at Skipton: where industrial Yorkshire meets the Dales.

Into the Yorkshire Dales National Park: the familiar limestone outcrop of Kilnsey Crag.

Above: The village of Burnsall, in Wharfedale, with the church at its heart.

Left: Bolton Abbey, Wharfedale, auspiciously sited on a bend in the river.

Above: A typical Dales scene of walls and field barns near Grassington.

Right: A limestone landscape, with the River Wharfe in the distance.

Springtime comes to Wharfedale – low light revealing lines of old field systems, known as 'lynchets'.

Springtime comes to Wharfedale – with a snow blizzard (in April!) making a monochrome moonscape out of a limestone pavement.

One of the Norber Erratics: boulders of Silurian slate left high and dry by glacial action on pedestals of limestone.

A cyclist pedals across the bridge into the Wharfedale village of Kettlewell.

Walkers on the Dales Way pass through the hamlet of Yockenthwaite.

The chimney of Cupola smelt mill, on the extensive lead-mining fields of Grassington Moor.

For a lot of people, a visit to Malham Cove is their first introduction to the Yorkshire Dales.

A clear road ahead for a cyclist in Malhamdale.

The wall-builders of Malham shunned squares and rectangles in favour of a more creative approach.

A train going south on the Settle-Carlisle Railway, across the 24 arches of Ribblehead Viaduct.

Above: The limestone landscape of Winskill Stones, near Settle, beneath a light dusting of snow.

Left: The 'picture postcard' village of Clapham, near Settle, and the footbridge over Clapham Beck.

The famous Three Peaks of Yorkshire comprise Ingleborough, Wernside and, here, Pen-y-ghent.

Ingleborough in winter, with a cap of cloud, viewed from Kingsdale.

The mist lifts to reveal the distinctive profile of Pen-y-ghent.

Inglebrough seen from 'the other side' – Coverdale – with morning mist still clinging to the valleys.

Above: The Pennine Way traverses Pen-y-ghent, which, at almost 700m, is the highest point that walkers have so far encountered on their walk.

Opposite: Halton Gill, an archetypal Dales hamlet in Littondale, backed up by fells.

Early summer in Littondale – sunlit fields backed up by limestone scars.

Above: A couple of walkers stroll through Arncliffe, another of Yorkshire's 'picture postcard' villages.

Overleaf: Hag Dike Farm, in Coverdale, marooned on the shores of a misty ocean.

Left: A farmhouse near Ravenseat in Birkdale, shrouded in mist.

Above: Cauldron Falls, near the village of West Burton in Bishopdale.

Above: Lambing time: a typical springtime scene in Wensleydale.

Left: A perfect day for sledging, in the fields around the Wensleydale market town of Hawes.

A simple pattern of walls and field barns near Burtersett.

The broad valley of Wensleydale, with some of the field barns that lend the Dales their distinctive character.

Above: The clouds part – for just a few seconds – leaving the village of Askrigg caught in the spotlight.

Left: Cotter Force: a staircase of water after summer showers.

Les Harker, and helping hands, in his farmyard near West Witton, Wensleydale.

Vernacular Dales architecture in the village of Thornton Rust.

Dent, a fascinating Cumbrian town that also happens to lie within the Yorkshire Dales National Park.

Above: A couple of inquisitive calves on Cam Fell, between Wharfedale and Wensleydale.

Left: Lockin Garth Falls, a beautiful little waterfall in Deepdale.

Farmers taking their vintage tractors for a spin at the weekend.

A pair of lambs pose obligingly, against Cam Fell, with Wild Boar Fell in the distance.

Above: A biker on a section of the Pennine Way between Cam Fell and Wensleydale.

Right: Looking north from Deepdale to the northern Dales.

The Georgian façades of Frenchgate, in Richmond, reflect the warm evening light.

Early summer in Swaledale, with the hamlet of Ivelet in the background.

Above: Patterns of walls and barns, looking down from Gunnerside to the flood-plain of the Swale.

Left: The beautiful old packhorse bridge at Ivelet, spanning the River Swale.

Above: Green fields around the village of Muker in early summer, before the first mowing.

Right: My favourite view in the Yorkshire Dales: looking down over the River Swale from lonely Crackpot Hall.

A walker retraces the route that lead miners would have taken, to the remote mines of Swinner Gill.

Fields make good neighbours in upper Swaledale.

The remains of Old Gang smelt mill, in a side-valley between Swaledale and Arkengarthdale.

Upper Swaledale – and a 'mother of pearl' sky – from the flank of Kisdon Hill.

The Methodist Chapel at Cautley, near Sedbergh, against a backdrop of the Howgill Hills.

I can't think of any building I love more than the Quaker Meeting House at Brigflatts, built in 1675.

Above: The interior of Brigflatts, simple and modest: the silence is almost tangible.

Right: Folds of the Howgill fells delineated by evening light.

Above: A close family group, looking from Firbank Fell towards the Howgills.

Left: The Yorkshire Dales National Park is left behind, as the Mallerstang Valley heads north towards Kirkby Stephen.

Nick Chetwood, signalman, on duty at Garsdale Station, on the Settle-Carlisle Railway.

A field barn beneath Mallerstang Edge, on the border between Yorkshire and Cumbria.

Above: Flags flutter on quad bikes, as they pass the army's firing range on Warcop Fell.

Right: A farmer and his dog drive a flock of sheep to new pasture, near Nateley.

Sheep graze by the ruins of Pendragon Castle, reputed to be the birthplace of King Arthur.

The road between Swaledale and Kirkby Stephen, rising through the mist towards the Pennine watershed.

A pair of walkers on the track up to Nine Standards Rigg, a distinctive landmark overlooking Kirkby Stephen.

Four of the nine cairns, known as the Nine Standards, which stand at 662 metres above sea level, on the route of Wainwright's Coast-to-Coast Walk.

An abandoned house on the high fells of the Pennine watershed.

The welcome sight that greets weary Pennine Wayfarers: Tan Hill Inn, which, at 527 metres, is the highest pub in the land.

Brough Castle, one of the five castles inherited in 1643 by the indomitable Lady Anne Clifford.

Brougham, another of the castles that Lady Anne restored; after she died here, in 1676, it fell into ruin again.

A shaft of sunlight picks out the façade of St Lawrence's church, in Kirkland, as a mighty storm brews over Cross Fell.

Dufton, another port of call for Pennine Wayfarers, as
they prepare for the rigours of the North Pennine hills.

Above: The elaborate sandstone water fountain in Dufton, against the conical shape of Dufton Pike.

Right: A pair of walkers pose in front of High Cup Nick, one of the geological highlights of the Pennine Way.

High Cup Nick, a classic U-shaped valley that offers a view from the North Pennines back down to the lush Eden Valley.

One of the many cairns – known locally as 'curricks' – to be found in the North Pennine uplands.

A sheep poses magisterially in front of Cross Fell, which, at 893 metres, is the highest point in the Pennines.

Above: A paramedic relaxes as the traffic heads down the A686, a notoriously dangerous – and very scenic – stretch of road.

Left: A tiny whitewashed cottage stands alone in the featureless fells around Hartside Top.

Alston, the 'capital' of the North Pennines, has claims to be the highest market town in England.

This solitary arch near Rookhope is all that now remains of a lead-smelting mill.

Above: Moles displayed on a fence in the North Pennines: visible evidence that the molecatcher has done his work.

Right: Evening comes to a lonely farmhouse on the fells to the north of Alston.

A wall snakes up a flank of Cold Fell – the altitude is more modest on the approach to Hadrian's Wall.

The wall, at Steel Rigg, built by Emperor Hadrian to mark the extent of his expansionist ambitions.

The fort at Birdoswald, near Gilsland: once home to a thousand Roman troops.